OLASTIC

ews

tion Readers

Earth

by
Christine Taylor-Butler

Children's Press®
A Division of Scholastic Inc.
New York Toronto London Auckland Sydney
Mexico City New Delhi Hong Kong
Danbury, Connecticut

These content vocabulary word builders
are for grades 1-2.

Consultants: Daniel D. Kelson, Ph.D.
Carnegie Observatories
Pasadena, CA
and
Andrew Fraknoi
Astronomy Department, Foothill College

Curriculum Specialist: Linda Bullock

Photo Credits:

Photographs © 2005: Corbis Images: 4 top, 4 bottom left, 11 (Matthias Kulka), 17 (Jim Sugar); Hawaii Volcanoes National Park via SODA: 4 bottom right, 15; NASA: back cover; Peter Arnold Inc./Astrofoto: 5 bottom right, 9 top; Photo Researchers, NY: cover (European Space Agency/SPL), 1, 5 top left, 5 bottom left, 9 bottom (Mehau Kulyk); PhotoDisc/Getty Images via SODA: 2, 5 top right, 7, 23; U.S. Department of Agriculture via SODA: 19.

Book Design: Simonsays Design!

Library of Congress Cataloging-in-Publication Data

Taylor-Butler, Christine.
  Earth / by Christine Taylor-Butler.
    p. cm. – (Scholastic news nonfiction readers)
  Includes bibliographical references and index.
  ISBN 0-516-24923-1 (lib. bdg.)
  1. Earth–Juvenile literature. I. Title. II. Series.
QE501.T35 2005
551.1–dc22
                              2005002419

1 2 3 4 5 6 7 8 9 10 R 14 13 12 11 10 09 08 07 06 05

CONTENTS

WORD HUNT

Look for these words as you read. They will be in **bold**.

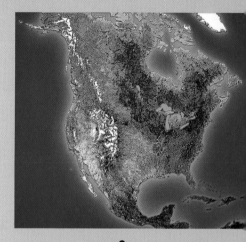

continent
(**kon**-tih-nuhnt)

island
(**eye**-luhnd)

lava
(**lah**-vuh)

4

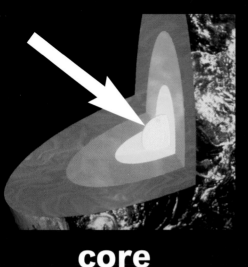

core
(kor)

Earth
(urth)

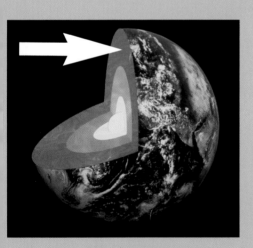

mantle
(**man**-tuhl)

solar system
(**soh**-lur **siss**-tuhm)

Earth!

You can eat the crust of a piece of bread.

But can you eat the crust of the **Earth**?

No. Earth's crust is made of rock.

Most of the Earth's crust is covered with water.

Earth is the only planet in the **solar system** with human life.

All life on Earth lives on the crust.

The crust is one of Earth's layers. It is the outside layer.

The **mantle** is under the crust.

The **core** is in the center of Earth.

solar system

Earth

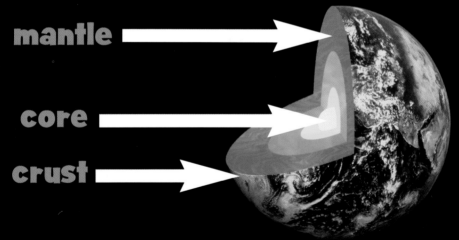

mantle

core

crust

Think of the crust of the Earth
like the eggshell of an egg.

Large parts of Earth's crust rise above the water.

These parts are called **continents**.

Smaller parts rise above water, too.

These parts are called **islands**.

People live on continents and islands.

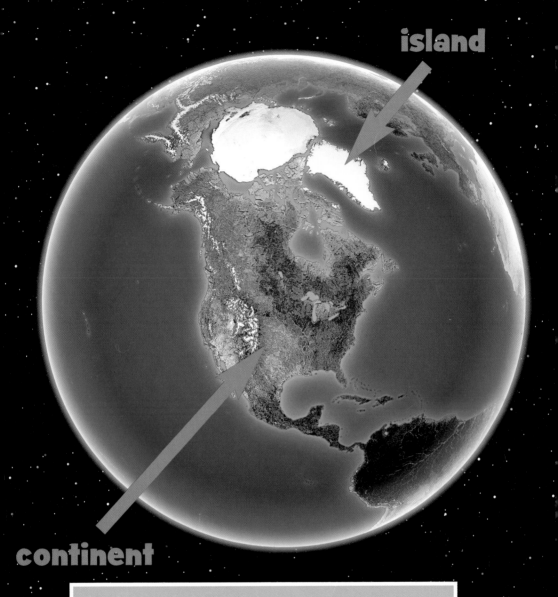

island

continent

Earth has seven continents and many islands. This continent is North America.

The Earth's crust is broken into many pieces, called plates.

These are not like dinner plates.

These plates are made of rock.

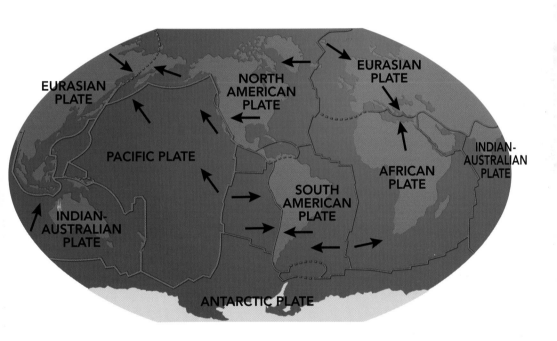

EURASIAN PLATE

NORTH AMERICAN PLATE

EURASIAN PLATE

PACIFIC PLATE

INDIAN-AUSTRALIAN PLATE

AFRICAN PLATE

INDIAN-AUSTRALIAN PLATE

SOUTH AMERICAN PLATE

ANTARCTIC PLATE

The red lines show the shapes of Earth's plates.

Earth's mantle is under the crust.

It is made of melted rock called magma.

Earth's plates float on the magma.

Magma that comes out of the Earth is called **lava**.

lava

Sometimes Earth's plates move.

This creates earthquakes.

Sometimes the crust pushes up.

This creates mountains.

Sometimes magma rises.

This creates a volcano.

Lava shoots out of this volcano.

We eat things that live on Earth's crust.

We eat things that grow in Earth's crust.

But we don't eat Earth's crust.

It would taste like dirt and rock!

Corn is one food that grows on Earth's crust.

Pluto

Uranus

Jupiter

Mar.

Mercury

EARTH

IN OUR SOLAR SYSTEM

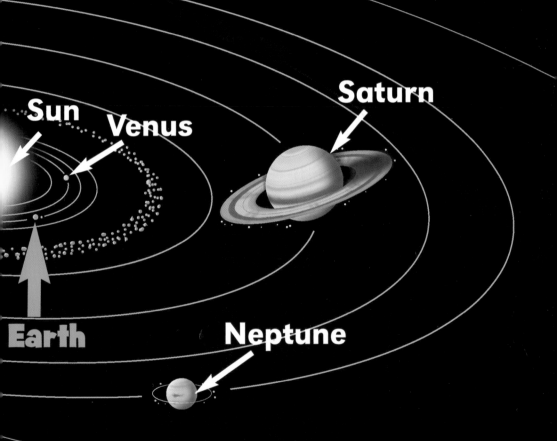

Sun

Venus

Saturn

Earth

Neptune

YOUR NEW WORDS

continent (**kon**-tih-nuhnt) a very large area of land; there are seven continents on Earth

core (kor) the center of Earth

Earth (urth) the planet we live on

island (**eye**-luhnd) a small area of land that rises above the water

lava (**lah**-vuh) hot magma that comes out of a volcano

mantle (**man**-tuhl) the layer between Earth's crust and the core

solar system (**soh**-lur **siss**-tuhm) the group of planets, moons, and other things that travel around the Sun

Earth Is an Amazing Planet!

A year is how long it takes a planet to go around the Sun. Earth's year = 365 days.

A day is how long it takes a planet to turn one time. Earth's day = 24 hours.

Earth has 1 moon.

Earth is more than 4 billion years old.

Earth is the only planet in the solar system

INDEX

FIND OUT MORE

Book:

Smithsonian Earth

Smithsonian Institution, James F. Luhr, Editor-in-Chief

DK Publishing, Inc., 2003

Website:

Solar System Exploration

http://sse.jpl.nasa.gov/planets

MEET THE AUTHOR:

Christine Taylor-Butler is the author of more than 20 books for children. She holds a degree in Engineering from M.I.T. She lives in Kansas City with her family where they have a telescope for searching the skies.